Journeys
in the
Mythic Sea

JIM HARTER
Journeys
in the
Mythic Sea

AN
INNERSPACE
ODYSSEY

Harmony Books/New York

I am grateful for the inspiration and support shown by many friends, which has made this book possible. I specifically wish to acknowledge the following for their contribution: Jean Letschert, David Singer, Esther Mitgang, Shyam Bhatnagar, Harish Johari, Barbara Vaccaro, Jacqueline Binder, Gert Van Der Helden, Terry Goodbody, Virginia Lyons, Marc Gevaert, Joan Hall, William Kaye, Tony Bloch, Don Rifkin, Colleen Haiber, Barbara Harter-Whitten, and my mother, Bennett Kerr. I thank all of you.

The following artwork has previously appeared in print: "A Vision of Apocalypse," "The Play of Opposites," "The Divine Metamorphosis," "The Game of Symbols," "Poet Tree," and "Ego Dream Death."

Published by Harmony Books, a division of Crown Publishers, Inc., One Park Avenue, New York, New York 10016 and simultaneously in Canada by General Publishing Company Limited.

HARMONY and colophon are trademarks of Crown Publishers, Inc.

Manufactured in the United States of America

Library of Congress Cataloging in Publication Data
Harter, Jim.
    Journeys in the mythic sea.
    1. Harter, Jim.   2. Geographical myths in art.
1. Title
NE539.H37A4   1985   769.92'4   85-910
ISBN 0-517-55756-8 (pbk.)

Book design by Ron McCutchan

10 9 8 7 6 5 4 3 2 1

First Edition

This book is dedicated to
the memory of the late
Wilfried Satty;
in grateful appreciation
for his friendship and
the inspiration that
his art has given me.

The Spell of Maya

Each of us has a dream that we pursue: a goal to be reached, a victory to be won, and then what? We go on to other dreams, and still others: a sequence that if we were to live eternally would stretch to infinity. To a Westerner such a thought might sound strange, but to one from the East it would be consistent with his traditional beliefs. There, man is seen as an eternal dreamer and dream chaser in a continuum that reaches both forward and backward beyond the limits of his present existence.

The world in which man lives is considered to be illusory and is given the name of Maya. Maya is frequently depicted as having feminine qualities. She is seen as the seductive or enchanting power of life that holds all living creatures in thrall. It is the fate of each soul to come to know Maya very intimately. The worlds around man, from the lowest to the highest, are all Maya: a pyramid of illusion. Yet, in this present age, man increasingly has created for himself a world of confusion and chaos, a dimension of bad dreams. He has lost his sensitivity to life, seeing only its surface but not its depths. Instead of Mother Maya, he sees only a dead planet, and in his greed rapes and despoils her, not knowing of the destructive wrath that will surely follow.

Maya is the dream theater and man is the actor in this theater. It is his higher destiny to lift her veils, to attune himself to her rhythms, and to learn her subtle mysteries. Maya is the goddess and the wise man is her lover.

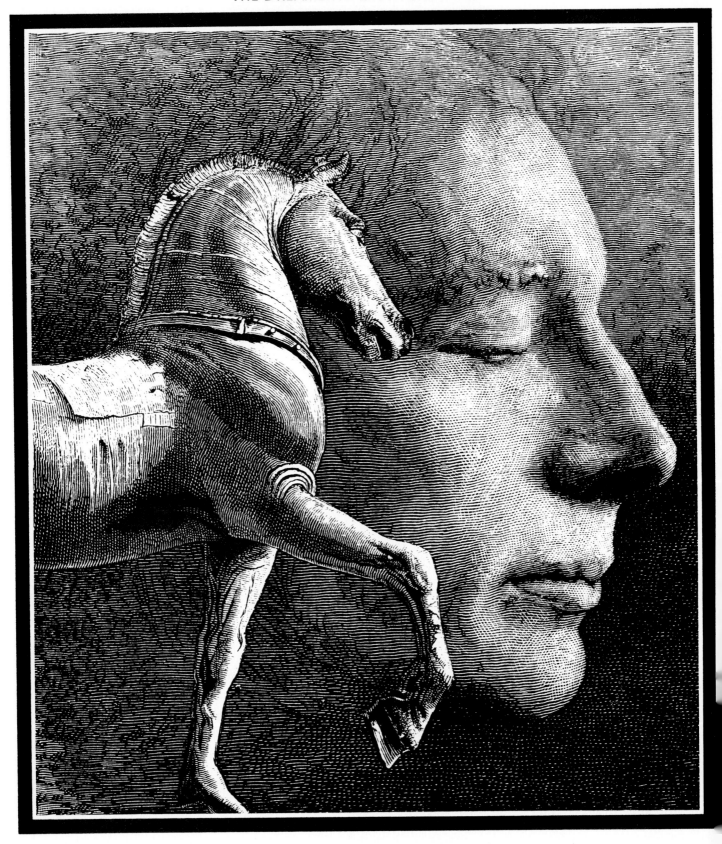

The Church of Machines

The Minister of Information

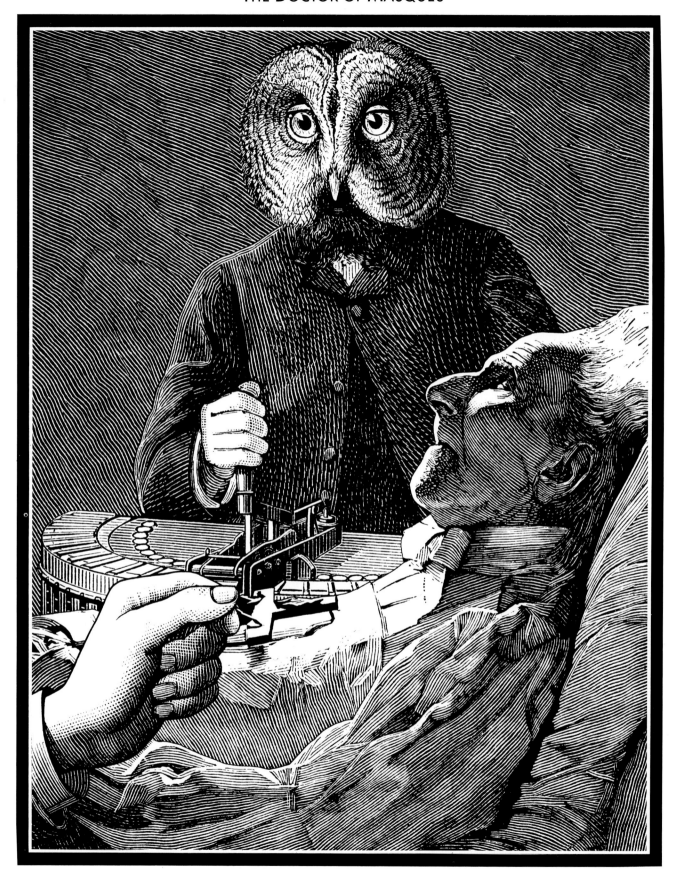

14

The Play of Opposites

Maya has both a creative and a destructive side and embodies all other opposites as well, such as everything and nothing, life and death, light and dark, good and evil, male and female, hot and cold, and up and down. The world in which we live is a focal point where countless polarities converge and interact. Man's destiny is to walk the narrow tightrope between them; balancing and harmonizing, he reaches a new synthesis of greater awareness.

With increasing wisdom, he awakens to the poetic dimension of reality. He sees the play of opposites everywhere. He learns the value of surrendering to the hidden flow of life: Its pleasures and pains have some secret purpose and are necessary food for the growth of his soul. Human greatness requires both the ability to balance strong contradictions and the inner strength and courage to undergo tremendous suffering. If he allows his life stream to flow unimpeded, it soon becomes a river, hurling him toward greatness.

MAN AND WOMAN, FIRE AND WATER, AIR AND EARTH

SELF AND EGO

The Divine Metamorphosis

Man moves through many worlds. He suffers in ignorance with the masses: Rising slowly, he acquires wealth and enjoys all the sensual pleasures of love and beautiful objects. He wields the reins of power and lives the life of the famous. Yet each of these worlds is bittersweet, and each is only a step in his climb up the holy mountain.

In time his heart opens up to Maya in her guise as the Muse. He is inspired in the arts and creates at a universal level, infusing his creations with all the experience of his previous lives. With infinite patience he climbs still higher, devoted to the selfless service and teaching of others. The river enters the sea, private life fades, ego dies, opposites unite, and the summit is reached. He explodes into a radiant world of divine light.

There is no psychological system in the West that adequately explains the phenomenon of sainthood. In the East, however, a saint is considered the end product of human evolution. There is a richer tradition of saintly existence in the East. Every saint is distinct, yet each shares common characteristics, such as an expanded capacity for wisdom, fearlessness, ecstasy, compassion, great sensitivity, an intense love for nature and his fellow human beings, healing abilities, psychic powers, and an ability to perform miracles. In essence, saints are very noble human beings.

The Primal Symphony

Kundalini City

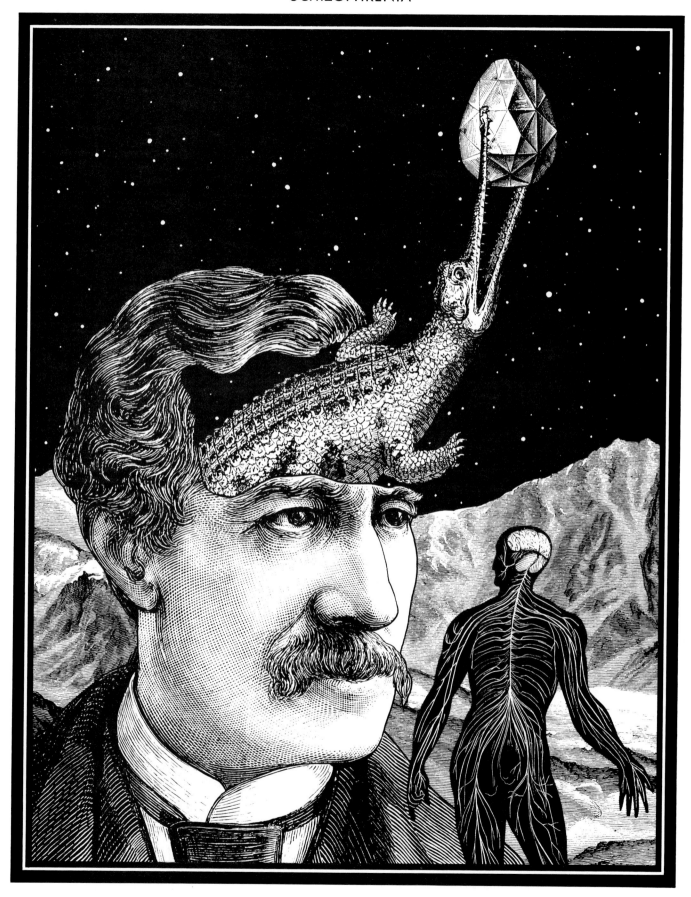

Visions of a Saintly Madman

The spiritual road toward divine vision is a progression like the climbing of a staircase where dreams turn into reality and each realization provides the base for a greater dream. The creative individual who possesses a universal vision has magnified his capacity to dream and has gained access to inner worlds of inspiration. To an even greater degree, a saint has this expanded awareness. His spiritual vision, fully awakened, penetrates through the illusory layers of his phenomenal existence into the timeless world beyond, a psychic dimension of infinite possibilities. This is the numinous world of the gods and heroes where life's primordial patterns, the archetypes, exist: where past, present, and all possible futures simultaneously converge. It is the most preciously guarded secret of the Goddess, revealed only to a few.

With this greater awareness, the world of phenomena acquires a new face. Behind its manifold diversity emerges a magnificent unity. All life has become process, a burning fire: the endless transmutation of matter into spirit, an endless world of suffering, yet everywhere infused with divine love and joy. The Saintly Madman begins to hear all of life singing, a hymn of praise, a hymn of sacrificial offering. All voices become one and all of life divine.

An Explanation of the Process

The medium of collage is unique among art forms. The artist takes preexisting pictures and uses them to project his own vision or fantasy into a new piece of work. It can be seen as a form of ecology: recycling old images for new uses. If visual images are combined imaginatively, it is possible for their impact to be magnified many times. In the interplay of symbolic content a new statement, a reflection of one's own psyche, emerges.

Collage can also be seen as a sort of alchemy where the integration of images transmutes the lower into the higher, where the whole represents a great increase over the sum of its parts. The power of this art form, and ultimately of any other, lies in its ability to cast a magical spell over its beholder.

The pictures in this book were composed of wood engravings from the late nineteenth century. Wood engraving was the primary illustration technique in printed media until about 1890, when halftone photo reproduction gradually took over.

I began to collect this material initially for creating psychedelic concert posters. The collection began in an old bookstore in San Antonio, Texas, in 1972. I also made three journeys to Europe in my quest. I used books and periodicals published primarily in the United States, England, France, and Germany. Source periodicals include *The Illustrated London News*, *La Nature*, *Harper's Monthly*, and *Le Tour Du Monde*. Other source material includes *Picturesque America*, *Brehm's Tierleben*, *Wood's Natural History*, and *Meyer's Konversational Lexikon*. I have also gathered material from many other sources, including books on astronomy, anatomy, geography, and geology.

Typically, when I sit down to compose a collage, I will place in front of me about fifty to one hundred precut images and background pictures. I then look for image combinations that have unexpected surprise elements. I pay special attention to selecting images that have a homogeneous engraving style so that they harmonize into a single composition. When a final combination of pictorial ingredients is achieved, everything is glued down in place. Further work is done after the collage is photographically enlarged to a size where defects can be touched up and other improvements made. The finished collage is a totally integrated picture that looks as though it were originally engraved that way.

JIM HARTER